G000090349

Created and published by Knock Knock
1635-B Electric Avenue
Venice, CA 90291
knockknockstuff.com

Illustrations by Gemma Correll

This book is a work of editorial nonfiction meant
solely for entertainment purposes. It is not
intended to create actual panic or serve as
psychological advice or counsel. In no event
will Knock Knock be liable to any reader for any
damages, including direct, indirect, incidental,
special, consequential, or punitive damages,
arising out of or in connection with the use
of the information contained in this book.
So there.

Every reasonable attempt has been made to
identify owners of copyright. Errors or omissions
will be corrected in subsequent editions.

ISBN: 978-160106488-2
UPC: 825703-50016-5

10 9 8 7

100 Reasons to Panic about Getting Married

KNOCK KNOCK
VENICE, CALIFORNIA

1.

You're afraid your partner is not "the one."*

*He's "the one" you're marrying.

2.

You'll spend too much on the wedding.*

*Your debt will be one of the first things that truly belong to you both.

3.

You haven't known each other long enough.*

*The surprises to come will keep the marriage fresh longer—or much, much shorter.

4.

You'll lose your sense of independence and adventurousness.

*The next time you find yourself hungover in a Tijuana jail, you'll have company.

5.

You'll inherit crazy relatives.*

*This will give you something to talk
about with the boring relatives.

6.

You'll have to agree on major purchases.*

*You can share the blame as well as the credit card.

7.

Evenings will be spent in front of the television in sweatpants.*

8.

People won't flirt with you anymore.*

*To some people, a wedding ring is an aphrodisiac.

9.

All your friends think you're making a huge mistake—but no one's telling you.*

*Someone always finds a way to tell you.

10.

You'll split up within the first year.*

*You could split up even if you don't get married. But then: no gifts or honeymoon.

11.

Your sex life will be boring.*

*This is what the Internet is for. You'll either get some good ideas or discover that there are worse things than boring sex.

12.

Your spouse will
turn out to be
a perv in the sack.*

13.

Your sex life will cease to exist.*

*Doesn't boring sex sound pretty good about now?

14.

You won't be able to relate to your single friends anymore.*

*Listening to their dating woes will make you want to stay married.

15.

Your spouse will turn out to be totally nuts.*

*Multiple personalities: it's like you're having an affair without cheating.

16.

You'll have to invite people you don't like to your wedding.*

*You'll need someone to sit
with Aunt Gladys and Uncle Morty.

17.

All you'll remember about the wedding is the stress it caused you.*

ARGH!!

*Conveniently, anti-anxiety meds can cause memory loss.

18.

You're an early bird. Your spouse is a night owl.*

*Afternoons will be a delight!

19.

Eventually, one of you will be attracted to someone else.*

20.

Your partner is a spoiled child in a grownup body.*

*Being married will be great
practice for having kids.

21.

You have to contend with someone else's fingernail clippings, hair clumps, and unsavory odors.*

*It's like *CSI*—in your own home!

22.

She always beats you at Scrabble.*

*You have someone to play Scrabble with.

23.

Your spouse will develop irritating habits or flaws.*

*They will balance yours out nicely.

24.

You won't be able to go on crazy spending sprees anymore.*

*You will, for things like appliances and life-insurance policies.

25.

You're Jewish.
She's Christian.
It will be
a disaster.*

*Christmas, Hanukkah,
and Purim! It's a win-win-win.

26.

Your spouse will be a lousy parent.*

*Well, at least you'll have the kid if
the whole marriage thing doesn't work out.

27.

You'll fight.
A lot.*

*Hello, makeup sex!

28.

Your parents will think you like your in-laws more than you like them.*

*It's about time your parents stepped up their game.

29.

Your partner will have debts you don't know about.*

*Or she'll have secret oil money.

30.

You won't agree on parenting styles.*

*Two kids: one for each of you to screw up.

31.

Your spouse will know that you actually poop.*

*Everyone poops.

32.

Your wedding will be ruined by drunk, fist-fighting cousins.*

*Your wedding will be one they'll never forget.

33.

Your partner's kids will hate you.*

*You'll be selflessly deflecting the hatred from their biological parent.

34.

Your spouse won't want to get rid of that hideous moose head.*

*That means you can keep some of your own hideous stuff.

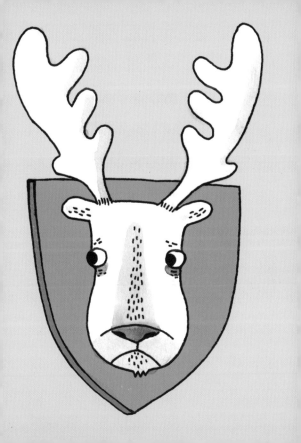

35.

You don't share the same political views.*

*Mary Matalin and James Carville
have made it work.

36.

You'll have to delete anyone you booty-called from your phone list.*

37.

You'll become a golf widow(er).*

*You'll have lots of time to hang out with
the single friends you never get to see anymore.

38.

Sharing a bank account means admitting how much you spend on your tin robot collection.*

*The display case was getting full anyway.

39.

Once you're married, you'll give up your loft downtown and move to the suburbs.*

*Well, the schools are much better out there.

40.

Registering for gifts just seems so...greedy.*

*When else can you tell people exactly what you want them to give you?

41.

You won't have your own personal space.*

*Why do you think they invented
indoor plumbing? So people would have
bathrooms in which to hide.

42.

Even if you go into the bathroom he's still out there.*

*When you decide you want to be around people again, you won't have to leave your house.

43.

You'll never go on another first date.*

*And never have to smile and nod your way through a meal with a stranger again.

44.

You'll be stuck with the same person forever.*

*You'll never have to go on a first date again.

45.

Your mother will take over the wedding.*

*Wedding planners are expensive.

46.

You'll need to check in if you're running late—like a teenager with a curfew.*

*Someone cares where you are. And what if you really *were* lying in a ditch somewhere?

47.

when she's sick, you'll have to take care of her.*

Tissues

*And when you're old, she'll change your diapers.

48.

Your spouse will hog the closet space.*

*Great excuse to leave
your clothes all over the place.

You'll turn into one of those couples that unintentionally dress in matching outfits.*

*It'll be that much easier to find each other when you get lost in a crowd.

50.

You'll be forever flipping the toilet seat down—or up.*

*You'll be forever getting a great bicep workout.

51.

You'll fight in front of the kids.*

*They'll think they live in their very own reality TV show.

52.

when she does the laundry, your white shirts end up pink.*

53.

Your husband could be a secret polygamist.*

*Sister wives help make up for your shortcomings.

54.

Your spouse's crazy ex will stalk you.*

*This will give you great fodder
for your blog or novel.

55.

You won't
be able to check
people out
anymore.*

*You can be chained up on the front porch
and still bark at other dogs.

56.

Divvying up the holidays between your families is like brokering an international peace treaty.*

57.

You won't have compatible culinary tastes.*

*There's always the food court.

58.

You'll have to listen to his music.*

THE CAT'S YOWL

*You'll learn to appreciate
that crap—or at least act like you do.

59.

A wedding ring is just another thing to worry about losing.*

*Or another item to happily pawn one day.

60.

Your spouse is too young for you.*

*You'll always feel young and spry.

61.

Your spouse is too old for you.*

*You'll always feel young and spry.

62.

Your partner will turn into his father (or her mother).*

*There are probably far worse relatives to take after—check out the family history.

63.

Your favorite TV shows are on in the same time slot.*

*All hail the DVR.

64.

Your spouse will want you to spend your vacation camping with Aunt Edith.*

65.

Your partner will
be resentful of
how much money
you make.*

66.

Your partner will be resentful of how little money you make.*

*At least one of you will have
plenty of cash to pay for marriage counseling.

67.

You're stuck with those nicknames 'til death do you part.*

*When you hear "Honeynugget?" at the grocery store, you're the only one who will answer.

68.

Your days of wild weekends must come to an end.*

*Your liver thanks you.

69.

A bag of chips and a six-pack will no longer be considered a well-balanced meal.*

70.

Your spouse's personality will change.*

*Could get worse, could get better.

71.

You'll be taken for granted.*

*What better opportunity to
indulge your passive-aggressiveness?

72.

Your spouse will have lousy decorating taste.*

*That's deliberately ironic kitsch.
At least, that's what you'll tell everyone.

73.

You'll hate his friends.*

*How bad can his taste be?
He picked you, after all.

74.

Making it official
means you'll be
part of the
establishment.*

*You'll be like secret agents trying to
destroy it from within.

75.

Your spouse won't let you bungee jump or run with the bulls.*

*Your life expectancy will take a thirty-year leap.

76.

He might go bald.*

77.

Your partner will try to change you.*

*People may like the new you a whole lot better.

78.

You'll loathe your in-laws.*

*They'll make you appreciate your parents more than ever.

79.

That statistic about 50% of marriages ending in divorce isn't reassuring.*

*You'll be motivated to prove it wrong.

80.

You feel oppressed by the terms "husband" and "wife."*

*You can always fall back
on the phrase "trusty sidekick."

81.

Merging two households means one of you has to give up your beloved sofa.*

*Welcome to the art of compromise.

82.

Now the pressure's really on to have a kid.*

*It's as good a time as any
to learn to change the subject.

83.

Your standards of cleanliness vary greatly.*

*A little dirt boosts the immune system.

84.

That story he told when you first met—the one that took ten minutes but showed that he was funny, brave, and kind? You'll be hearing it the rest of your life.*

*At some point, your hearing will start to go.

85.

You have to remember his family's birthdays, food allergies, and shoe sizes.*

*Remembering dates and other trivia prevents dementia.

Your spouse won't give up her workaholic ways.*

*You won't get bored with each other if she is never around.

87.

Your spouse will lose his job and become a couch potato.*

*The spouse who stays home has to do the laundry and pay the bills. That's the deal.

88.

Once you're married, the romance will disappear.*

*The romance may disappear,
but the half-hearted gift of drugstore chocolate
on February 14th is a sure thing.

89.

Making dinner means accommodating your picky tastes— and hers.*

*It also means you're not cooking—or eating—solo.

90.

Your spouse will find out exactly how much debt you have.*

*Maybe she can help you
improve your money management skills.

91.

Life will be reduced to cleaning the house, making dinner, and playing bridge with the neighbors.*

*You'll be living in a 1950s TV show, so that will be nice.

92.

You hate watching football, college basketball, and hockey.*

*But it's the perfect excuse to eat all the chips and seven-layer dip you want.

93.

Your spouse is only pretending to be well-adjusted.*

*It's the unknowns that make a marriage exciting.

94.

Your in-laws and parents won't like each other.*

*Imagine if they joined forces. There'd
be no end to the meddling they could achieve.

95.

The forecast for your wedding day? Rain.*

JUST MARRIED

*It can only get better from there. Probably.

96.

What if this one doesn't last either?*

*You'll have at least one thing
in common with Elizabeth Taylor.

97.

Heading to the bedroom means actually going to bed.*

*There's still the kitchen, the bathroom, the guest room, and the garage.

You'll be left at the altar.*

*The cake and gifts: all yours.

99.

You sometimes
wish he were
an orphan so you
didn't have to deal
with his family.*

*They produced the person you love.
And don't you forget it.

100.

You'll become a smug married person who makes comments like, "Well, when you get married you'll understand."*

*You're now a member of a special (albeit annoying) club.

*don't worry.
It's worth it.